Waking Up to This Moment

The Essential Meaning of BREEMA

Only this moment exists.

Also from Breema Center Publishing

Books:

Freedom Comes from Understanding: Insights for Meaningful Life

Breema and the Nine Principles of Harmony

Every Moment Is Eternal: The Timeless Wisdom of Breema

Self-Breema: Exercises for Harmonious Life (second edition)

Freedom Is in This Moment: 365 Insights for Daily Life

Audio CDs:

Waking Up to This Moment: The Essential Meaning of Breema

Freedom Comes from Understanding: Insights for Meaningful Life

Breema and the Nine Principles of Harmony

Waking Up to This Moment

The Essential Meaning of BREEMA

by Jon Schreiber

Breema Center Publishing
Oakland, California

Breema Center Publishing
6076 Claremont Avenue
Oakland, CA 94618

510-428-0937
Fax 510-428-9235
email: center@breema.com
website: www.breema.com

Photo Credits:
Front cover: PureStock, © Superstock, licensed via Fotosearch
Interior pages: Sibila Savage, Mark Kitaoka, Tracy Martin
Back cover: Joy Faye Rowan

Printed in USA

ISBN 978-1-930469-04-4

Library of Congress Control Number: 2011923877

Breema® and Self-Breema® are service marks of the Breema Center.

This book is for educational purposes only and is designed to familiarize the reader with basic principles of Breema. It is sold with the understanding that the publisher and author are not engaged in rendering medical or other professional health service via the book and its contents. The reader must clearly understand that Breema bodywork can be properly learned only in a live setting from a Certified Breema Instructor. In order to become a Breema Practitioner, completion of the Breema Center Certification Program is required.

The purpose of Breema is Self-understanding.

I hope the material in this book,
which comes from classes taught at the Breema Center,
will increase your desire for Self-understanding,
because that's the foundation of all understanding.

Introduction

Breema is the activity of the body when *I am present*. You study Breema to study yourself. The purpose of Breema's philosophy and of Breema bodywork is to support you in the direction of Self-understanding.

You cannot separate Breema bodywork or Self-Breema exercises from the philosophy of Breema. And the philosophy of Breema cannot be separated from the philosophy of Existence.

Breema bodywork and Self-Breema exercises are precious vehicles for gaining practical experiences that support us to bring body, mind, and feelings together and become present. This is the requisite step that we need to take again and again in the lifelong process of discovering and fulfilling the purpose and meaning of our life.

If this book is your introduction to Breema, you can find some indication here of the depth of Breema's philosophy and principles. If you experience an inner resonance with what you read, I hope you will have the opportunity to experience receiving a Breema bodywork session and also have the chance to learn Breema bodywork and Self-Breema exercises.

If you are already a student of Breema or a Certified Breema Practitioner or Instructor, you can draw inspiration and practical guidance for your ongoing practice of Breema bodywork and for self-study. There is a Breema bodywork sequence called "Understanding Gives the Highest Nourishment." I hope that every time you open this book, your desire for Self-understanding is nurtured.

Jon Schreiber

You and the Nine Principles
are not two separate things.
In the moment you taste your existence,
you are manifesting the Nine Principles.

The Nine Principles of Harmony

The Nine Principles of Harmony are the distillation and expression of Breema's comprehensive philosophy and understanding of the universal laws of Existence. They support us to move in the direction of Self-understanding.

The principles themselves are the essential facets of the Law of Unity. All nine principles exist within each principle, and all nine can be discovered within every harmonious phenomenon and in every movement towards greater harmony.

You and the Nine Principles are not two separate things. In the moment you taste your existence, you are manifesting the Nine Principles.

The Nine Principles of Harmony

BODY COMFORTABLE

When we look at the body, not as something separate, but
as an aspect of a unified whole, there is no place for discomfort.

NO EXTRA

To express our True nature, nothing extra is needed.

FIRMNESS AND GENTLENESS

Real firmness is always gentle. Real gentleness is always firm. When we are
present, we naturally manifest firmness and gentleness simultaneously.

FULL PARTICIPATION

The most natural way of moving and living is with full participation. Full participation
is possible when body, mind, and feelings are united in a common aim.

MUTUAL SUPPORT

The more our Being participates, the more we are able to support life and recognize
that Existence supports us. Giving and receiving support take place simultaneously.

NO JUDGMENT

The atmosphere of nonjudgment gives us a taste of acceptance of ourselves
as we are in the moment. When we come to the present, we are free from judgment.

SINGLE MOMENT/SINGLE ACTIVITY

Each moment is new, fresh, totally alive.
Each moment is an expression of our True nature, complete by itself.

NO HURRY/NO PAUSE

In the natural rhythm of life energy, there is no hurry and no pause.

NO FORCE

When we let go of assumptions of separation, we let go of force.

14. *Before Celebration*

- Recipient is supine.

- Stand on heels.

- Come to sitting cross-legged facing diagonally toward recipient's left foot.

- Pick up the left foot with your left hand under the heel and your right hand on the dorsum.

- Bring your left heel to support under your left hand.

- With both hands still holding the foot, lean back and slightly to your right to gently stretch the foot.

- Repeat this gentle stretch two more times.

- Still holding the heel with your left hand, bring your right hand to recipient's anterior leg, just below the knee—your thumb medial and your fingers lateral, in the natural channels on either side of the shin.

- Sit between the feet and hold the dorsi for three breaths.

- Brush to the toes and off to release, and

- Bow.

These notes are for review use only by Certified Breema Instructors and by students who receive a copy from an instructor after learning the sequence in a class. To assimilate both the form and essence of any Breema sequence, classroom study with a Certified Instructor is necessary.

the natural channels on either side of the shin—from just below the knee to the foot and along the lateral edges of the foot to the toes.

- Repeat the lean-hold-release two more times.

- Bring your right hand to hold the ball of the foot and tap down the anterior left leg with your left hand—alternating palm-up / palm-down—from just below the knee to the toes, and brush off.

- Repeat two more times.

- Still holding the ball of the foot with your right hand, brush with your left hand from the knee down the anterior left leg to the toes and off, three times.

- Holding the foot with both hands, lean back to stretch the leg.

- Lower the leg to the floor and turn to sit facing diagonally toward recipient's right foot.

- Switching the left / right use of your hands and legs, repeat everything on the right leg.

When Body, Mind, and Feelings
Come Together

Breema relates to health in the real sense, in the universal sense. In the wholeness of yourself, you are healthy. The more you understand this, the more real your practice of Breema bodywork becomes. When you place your hand on the recipient's body, this background is there to support both you and the recipient. Instead of just having a mechanical exchange, your Being can participate.

You can't separate Breema bodywork from the philosophy of Breema. They are necessary ingredients of each other.

When body and mind unite, our feelings can join in and become a great support. When we do Breema with our body, mind, and feelings engaged, we see that something is missing in the way we usually live.

When we get out of bed in the morning, we lie down in our psychological bed and sleep there all day. We look at things without seeing them, so we react to life.

But when body, mind, and feelings come together, we begin to live our life. Every Breema sequence, when practiced with the principles of Breema, gives us a new possibility.

By practicing Breema bodywork and Self-Breema daily, and working with the Nine Principles, we may come to the point where we see that every movement of the body could be Breema, every movement could be Self-Breema. Then you could manifest Breema in every aspect of your life, not only when you do bodywork.

A New Posture Towards Life

The purpose of practicing Breema is to bring you to the present, and support you to remain present.

If we recognize what the human body means—what it took for the universe to create this magical form—then we have the highest respect for it. If you practice Breema bodywork and Self-Breema, you see how much the body is respected. You have to be connected to yourself to do Breema; that much the body is respected.

From there, all the wisdom of Breema arises. Don't try to heal, don't try to fix, because as soon as you want to do that, you come to your mechanical mind and manifest something you don't understand. From the mechanical level, you try to fix something universal. Every one of us is self-developing. You don't need to develop someone else. Develop yourself!

Always be grateful. There is not one movement in Breema that isn't nurturing. Placing your hand on the body with any of the Breema principles alive is sufficient. That which is present nurtures your body, and nurtures the entirety. So just have this one aim always—to become present when you do Breema. Or wherever you are, for that matter.

We all have so many things in our mind—business, home, family, friends, so many obligations. While you are practicing Breema, accept that these few minutes are only for you. This time is yours.

We need Breema because we need a new posture towards life. If we examine our usual posture, we find that it fits under the heading of living in the past and future, of not knowing who we are. It's easy to see that this posture is not what we wish. And we are caught in it because we haven't found an alternative.

Breema offers us the possibility of having a new posture that tells us: "Let go of the thought of separation. You are not a separated something. You are part of one whole unified Existence."

With this new posture, you can have new thoughts and new feelings. You can wish to have a balanced, harmonious relationship between your mind, your feelings, and your body. When mind, feelings, and body are in harmony, you can have a harmonizing influence on your surroundings.

In your daily activities, do things with Full Participation. That's part of having a new posture. Do what you do with Single Moment/Single Activity—that's a new posture. It doesn't matter how much you have to do. When you start, you do one thing at a time. When you do one thing at a time, the thought of all the rest you have to do isn't draining your energy. You are fully participating in one single activity. Then the one thing you're doing generates enough energy for you to do the next thing.

When you see that your mind, feelings, and body are conditioned, you're on the right track. You're on the road to discovering that you're not what you think you are. Then you have the possibility to eventually have a new posture, new thoughts, new feelings, and a new relationship to your life. Don't get caught in what you have been or what you think you're going to be. Leave that alone. Be present, and you lessen your identification with the past and future.

Breema gives you a chance to discover that it's possible to relate to another human being with your whole Being participating. You can be filled up with well-wishing. You practice one Breema sequence and you see your fear of life decreases. Your fear of others decreases. You become more familiar with this machinery called body. What is its purpose? Why do we have life?

Breema is a model for living a harmonious life. Do one Self-Breema in the morning, and you will see the effect it has on your life.

The universe is like a necklace with many beads. Milky Way, sun, Earth, moon, human beings, science, philosophy—all of these are beads. But there is one thread that passes through all of them. It doesn't matter how many beads there are, one thread connects them to each other. We feel disconnected from everything in life because we've lost our connection to the thread. That thread is the dynamic of life that passes through everything every moment. What is this dynamic? Where does it come from? From the Absolute, and it passes through everything that exists. It is Awareness, and at the same time it is also Consciousness, energy, and matter.

If you understand this thread, the meaning of birth and death is easy to understand. When a light bulb burns out, nothing happens to the electricity. The cycle of birth and death is part of the process of Existence, and we are all going through it. We have this uniform called "body," and when we finish this school we leave the uniform behind, and we call that "death."

There is science. There is religion. They are ingredients of life. But if you get caught in any of the ingredients, no matter how great they may seem, all you did was get caught. Whatever comes to you in life, you need to translate into something practical, something for your daily life, something that supports you to know *I exist*. And fortunately, this has a very easy beginning—just "get Breema in your body." That means becoming familiar, through many experiences of receiving and giving Breema, with the taste that begins with body-mind connection. To the extent you get Breema in your body, the cotton comes out of your ears and you can hear, because you need Being-participation in order to hear truth.

What you know about Breema, you have to manifest. You have to manifest it in touch, in movement, in words. Breema is a process of transformation. But you don't see how you are being transformed unless you manifest it.

Why do you do Breema? To unify yourself and support life. With our eyes, we see form, texture, and color. We are totally identified with the obvious. We don't see the flow of the life force. But when you do Breema, you may experience it and so may the recipient. We need to see that we are not just "Mr. Head." We need to know we have a body. Body-mind connection is not just a phrase. It's a magnificent way of life. "Whole body/whole mind" is a direction for life. When you have Breema in your body, then when you move your hand, something takes place, because your whole body and whole mind are participating. When you sit, you are sitting. When you walk, you are walking. You have Being-participation.

Your Being Is Never in the Past

To the extent you are available at this moment, you are doing Breema. It's as simple as that. If you keep this direction clear for yourself and always work with it, you can come to a taste—the taste of being present.

Instead of being drawn to the past or future, where you have been conditioned to live, it's possible to live your life with meaning and purpose in the present. But for that, Being-participation is needed. And your Being is never in the past, never in the future.

When your Being participates, you are simple. You don't have extra. Body is comfortable. You have a relationship of mutual support with all life. Everything you do is Single Moment/Single Activity. There is No Hurry/No Pause. Firmness and gentleness are simultaneously present. In the moment, you are free from past and future, free from time and space, yet with acceptance of them.

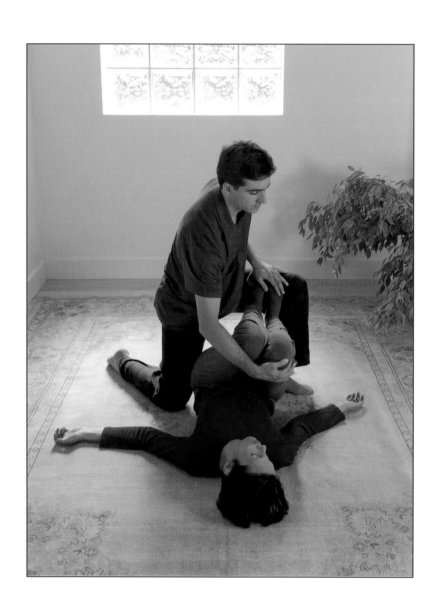

You do Breema to become present. Your aim is to taste *I exist*. That's all. You're not trying to say I am dexterous, I am good or bad, I know less, or I know more. Knowing *I exist* is sufficient. At the presence of the *I* that exists, all your thoughts about yourself lose their significance. That's how Breema is. There's no separation between practitioner and recipient. There's just Existence revealing itself moment after moment. Even the word "Breema" isn't there. There's just *is*.

Whole Body/Whole Mind

The first aim of Breema is to bring whole body/whole mind together. When you work with that, you learn a lot about yourself. You see how rare those moments are when whole body/whole mind are working together. You discover that you can't just decide you want that, and then it happens. Somewhere along the line, you find out that you are not master of yourself. You're not what you think you are.

When you get Breema *in your body,* you have something you didn't have before—a supportive atmosphere within yourself. That atmosphere is formed by organized knowledge that all fits together, combined with your own experiences and tastes of *there is a body.* These give you an inner organization that supports you to be present more often.

Breema's Nine Principles bring you in harmony with your True nature. The Law of Constant Change affects your mind, feelings, and body, and their activities. But in Awareness there is no change. Awareness simply is aware. In Awareness, you can see your life against the background of a permanent, unchanging Existence. Your True nature is the reality of yourself—your home in the entirety, your unseparated Being-existence.

If you relate to the recipient mentally, you're not fully participating. If you relate emotionally, you're not fully participating. If you relate physically, that's not Full Participation either. Because no one is actually there to participate.

In your mind, you are just a thought, not you. In your emotions, you are just sentiment, not you. Your body has sensations, but they're not you. We don't really know what the body is, what the feelings are, or what the mind is. Knowing doesn't belong to one part. It has to be full, it has to be complete. Fragmented knowledge doesn't give you what you need. Mind, feelings, and body have to participate together. Full Participation gives you a direction that leads toward self-knowledge.

When you are present, you can relate, you can participate in life because your Being is participating.

You are doing Breema. Your hand is on someone's body, and your body is leaning. The less identified you are with this hand, with this body, with this role, with this separated "me," the more Conscious energy flows. And through the flow of Conscious energy, you *taste* that you *exist*. That is Breema.

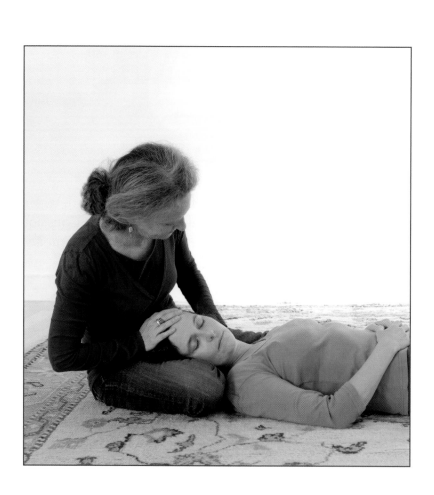

To manifest Breema, no extra is needed. What is extra? Anything that's not needed in this moment. Breema is not a technique, not something you learn. It's something you *are*. You have to learn a lot in order to let go of what you think you are and *be* what you are.

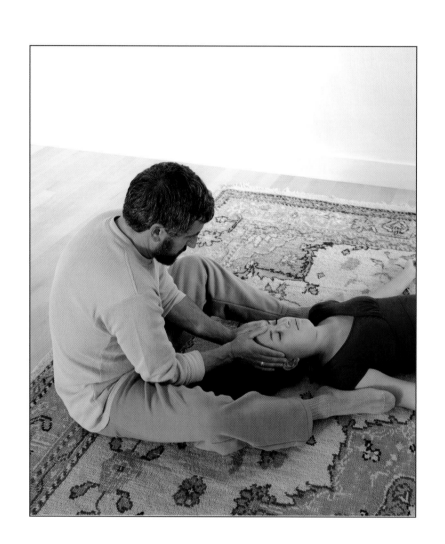

Moment after moment, you are in unity with the entirety. To know that, you need to be present. The truth is that you *are* present. The only effort that's needed is to let go of extra. There's one whole unified Existence, inclusive, undividable. All separation is imaginary. The direction is always from complication towards simplicity, from diversity towards unity. That doesn't mean denying diversity and trying to find unity. It just means opening up to receive the fact of your own existence, which is always in unity.

To Be Alive
Means to Be in the Present

You're practicing Breema. It's not about what you are doing. It's about *how are you* while you're doing it. The emphasis is not on the sensations of touch or any other sensation your sense organs can communicate to you. *Breema is the activity of the body while you are present.*

Your thoughts are always in the past and future. But your mind could become an instrument that has a job to do. You can ask your mind, time after time, to remain with the process of inhalation and exhalation. When it goes off somewhere, bring it back to register inhalation and exhalation. That harmonizes both your body and your mind.

When you practice Breema, you have a direction: "I wish to be available." The first step is to see you're not. You have to see you're always lost in thoughts, in feelings, in associations. Your mind is always in the past or future.

If you can see that you're not really here, that you're not present, you're on the right road, provided you wish to see that in acceptance.

In truth, you *are* here. All you need is to recognize that's so, but not in your thoughts. You recognize it in the taste of being present.

If you let go of extra, if you drop your concepts and just do Breema, there is an atmosphere in which both the recipient and you are accepted. In acceptance, you are both supported.

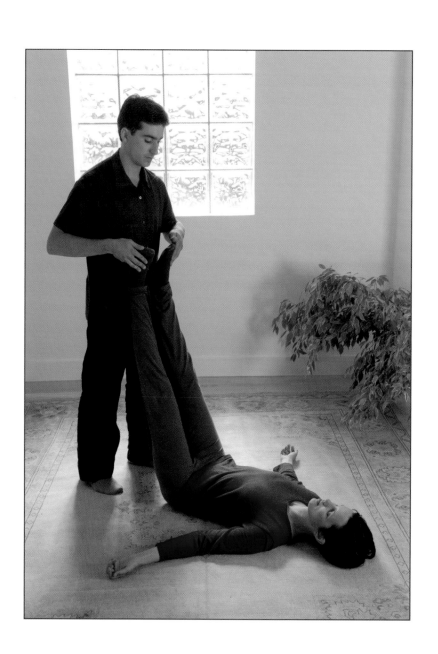

To have Full Participation, you need knowledge and Being. If you *are,* but you don't know what to do, you can't participate fully. If you know what to do, but you don't have Being, you can't do what you know. The body is the "ground" where you can experience the *taste* of understanding, which is the unification of knowing and Being.

Full Participation means entering into the understanding of the *is*-ness of yourself in this moment, through the taste of *I am*.

When we are inside our head, having random thoughts and walking through life, we are not living life. To be alive means to be in the present. In the present, you taste life within yourself.

First you have to taste *there is a body*. When you taste *there is a body,* you've come out of your thoughts. You directly taste that something exists. That "something" is you in this body. This is what it means to know you have a body. You are not your body, but there is a body. And you taste your existence in this body. When you go home, you don't think you are the room you're in.

When you see you are not this body, you drop your identification with the body. Your fear of life disappears.

Before you had this body, you existed. After your body goes back to the soil, and you return this "uniform" to the school of the Earth, you will still exist. In order to know that, you need to wake up.

Breema Is Existence Manifesting Itself

We practice Breema to practice the principles—Body Comfortable, Full Participation, Single Moment/Single Activity, No Judgment. What they really mean is acceptance of yourself in any given moment. The more you can accept yourself, the less attached you are to your concepts about yourself. If you let go of concepts, you simply *are*. The you that exists is not separate from the totality of everything that exists. That's why we say Breema is Existence manifesting itself.

Say you're standing in the street. People walk back and forth, coming and going. You don't have to go with them. That's how your thoughts are. You don't have to get involved and go with them. Mind has thoughts. Feelings feel. Your senses have sensations. They're always there, in their own dimension. But you can live *your* life.

Where does your life start? Where does the water you see flowing in the river start? From snow melting on the mountain peak. You can't look at a section of the river and say that it's the whole river. By the time you say it, the water you looked at has moved on, and new water has taken its place. So how can you say this is your life, this seventy or eighty years in this container? How can you separate it from the flow of life? You are like a drop of water flowing in the river. There are countless drops of water flowing from the source and eventually returning to the source. That's the process of existence of the universe. Everything is made of light. Everything comes from light and returns to light.

Something real exists, beyond time and space, beyond name and form. That's what gives reality to time and space, name and form, color and texture, to everything that is. When you're connected to that source, you are real. Your body is real. Everything you see is real, because you don't try to separate yourself. You are part of the process, and you exist. A drop of water in the river is welcome to be a drop. In the flow of the river, it has reality. When you're connected to the Totality, you exist. But this time, for real. Not in imagination. And you don't need anyone or anything to validate it for you, because the taste of it is undeniable.

You want to know who you really are. In the moment you can say "I am" and taste the reality of that statement, you exist with the Totality, and everything is real with you. There is *one* reality, *one* Existence. There is *one* energy, *one* Consciousness, *one* Awareness. In this one unified Existence, you exist. And you can know it, because Being, knowing, and understanding all unite in a moment of *I am*-ness.

Why do we have a hard time getting this? Because we've been miseducated to take ourselves as if we're separate. You believe you are your name, you believe you are your body. But how could that be you? Your name and form are good for seventy or eighty years. If that were you, you'd be a temporary existence that becomes non-existence. But existence cannot be temporary. It is permanent. Whatever exists, exists forever, eternally. Beyond past and future. Present, moment after moment. That is your real existence.

To know you exist,
a different education is needed.
"Knowing" by thought isn't sufficient.
*Knowing by **taste** is needed.*

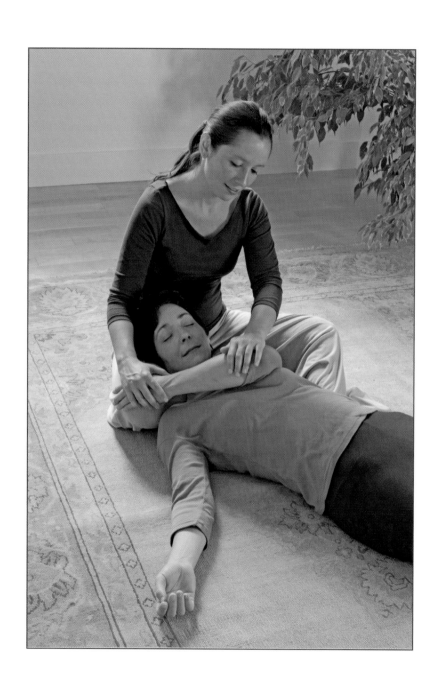

We are always in the past or future. We try to construct something we can call "present," something in between the past and future. But that can never be found. When we "get there," it's already past. Before we come to it, it's the future.

As long as we think in time and space, we can't enter reality. Because reality belongs to the Timeless dimension of Existence, to the moment. The entire past and future are present in this moment. To benefit from the past or the future, we need to be present. Because the taste of *I-am*-ness is found only in this moment.

Practicing Breema with the desire to be present, you have the possibility to come to taste. When you have body-mind connection, you see that you and the body are two different phenomena. You have a chance to see you are not this mind, not this body. You are not your sensations, not your feelings. Then what are you? You are that which is *conscious* of mind, feelings, body, and sensations. This realization becomes your first taste of freedom.

Your Home Is the Entire Cosmos

In the entire universe, there is no life without form, and no form without life. Of course, there are many dimensions of life and form.

Finer consciousness needs a form proper to it. Why do you so rarely have a moment of being conscious? Because you do not have an instrument that's fine enough to contain that Conscious energy.

One of the purposes of practicing Breema is to prepare your machinery—your body, mind, and feelings—to have the capacity to receive finer consciousness. You are making yourself a more receptive vehicle for consciousness. When you become totally receptive, you can see diversity within unity, and unity in diversity. You see the part unseparate from the whole, and the whole unseparate from the part.

With our eyes we see the body as an object, because we are slaves to our sense organs. We think that what our senses communicate to us is how things really are. At some point, you may discover it's not so. Your senses tell you that you are this physical body. But at the presence of finer consciousness, you will see that the body is just a tool given to you to use. If you think you are this body, you're like a gardener thinking he is a shovel.

Your mind is a tool, but you identify with it as "you." Your body and your feelings are tools, but you identify with them as "you." Because of that identification, your world shrinks and becomes the world of "me" and "mine," and you suffer.

By working with Breema, you may start to become less identified with "me" and "mine." You open up a bit to the bigger picture.

Being on this Earth, in this body, you could experience that your home is the entire cosmos. You live in the Totality of everything that exists, unseparated.

To come to that, you first need to make a connection between your body and your mind. When they become connected and remain connected for a while, the feelings come in, and you receive the presence of a new, finer energy. As long as mind, feelings, and body remain together and function in harmony, you remain receptive to Conscious energy.

Breema works with the body
not only as matter and energy.
It also relates to it as
Consciousness and Awareness.

Don't allow yourself to think the recipient needs something, and that you are going to give it to them. Throw those ideas out the window! Don't try to heal them or make them more balanced. The moment you place your hand on their body, accept the unity of the recipient and yourself, because that's the truth.

When you taste your own Being-existence, every manifestation of your body is Breema. The presence of Consciousness in you is what gives support. Your hand is not doing bodywork. It's a representative of the entirety. The entirety is touching the entirety. Life is giving to life.

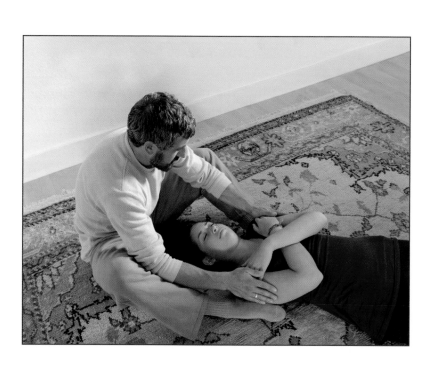

When you come to taste, you're in a dynamic relationship with your body, with your environment, and with yourself. And that's how you actually exist—always in relationship.

When you have taste, you have an inner atmosphere. That's your actual connection to your existence. You get Breema in your body by coming to taste again and again. Gradually, you establish a relationship to taste. That allows you to experience a natural confidence when you do Breema, because when taste is present, you are connected to that inner atmosphere. When you are leaning, when you are holding, when you stretch, when you move, you are supported by that inner atmosphere. That makes it Breema.

When taste is present, whatever you do is Breema. Practicing Breema sequences supports you to come to taste. But just following the form doesn't mean much if you are in the past or future. The form becomes supportive when *you* are there to follow it!

Life Is Giving to Life

Practicing Breema, you have an opportunity to know you have a body. The moment your body, mind, and feelings come together, you are moving towards becoming free from the concepts of "me" and "mine," and suffering diminishes. Life is giving to life. Existence is manifesting itself.

Your hand and your body are obviously separate from the recipient's body. You're not them, they're not you. But that just refers to the dimension of you that is matter-energy. In Consciousness and Awareness, you can see diversity is simply an aspect of unity. When you practice Breema, the recipient's life energy and your life energy are connected and support each other. You are both receiving from the same source.

But when Consciousness is not present, you want everything to be a certain way, based on your ideas and concepts. That makes you manipulative. When you're practicing Breema, don't believe the recipient needs your help, and you are the person who can help them. The most you can do for them is to be receptive yourself. That invites the recipient's receptivity, which is something that can help.

We think we know ourselves. We think we know who we are, but we don't. We have two aspects. One is the "child of Existence." That's the nature we were born with, given to us by Existence. The other is the "child of society." That's our acquired nature. We acquired it through our education—through contact with our parents, friends, teachers, and from everything we've seen, read, and heard. The child of Existence is our original nature. As we grow up, we acquire the child of society through education and imitation.

The child of society perceives everything through the distorted lens of the mind, so it doesn't recognize truth. The child of society grows to the extent that it completely covers the child of Existence. So we believe we are the child of society. Ask anyone what they want from life, and you'll see who answers. They want success, wealth, possessions, admiration, fame. The child of society is convinced that it is separated, and it acts as though it is. It likes to accumulate many name-tags, to distinguish itself from others.

Breema is something we do to prepare ourselves for the further development of the child of Existence. That's why the aim of practicing Breema and working with the Nine Principles is to be present. When we have many tastes of being present, we become available to benefit by the essential meaning of Breema.

Breema supports us to become less identified with our conditioning, with the child of society. Experiences of body-mind connection support the child of Existence. As we become less and less identified with our false self-concepts, our life becomes more meaningful.

Understanding is universal. It applies always and everywhere. Life never manifests the way we expect it to. If you understand that, then you don't have expectations. Free from association, you see what is. When you taste *I am*, you see with the light of Consciousness, and you have the ability to respond in the way that's needed.

The joy of doing Breema expresses itself in your entirety. You are not doing Breema—you *are* Breema. You are that which you are expressing. Putting your hand on someone's shoulder or picking up a cup becomes Existence manifesting itself. To get the actual taste and meaning of Breema, nothing is better than working with the Nine Principles. If you get Breema only in the form of the bodywork or Self-Breema exercises, you haven't benefited fully by what Breema has to offer. Breema is a universal principle, given to you to bring to your daily life. Everything you do could be Self-Breema or Breema. When you shop, when you eat, when you walk, when you talk, there could be an inner atmosphere that supports you to manifest in harmony. Don't wait until you have somebody to work on to practice Breema. Whenever your body is manifesting, that manifestation could become Breema.

Accept the condition of your body, whatever it is. As soon as you accept it, you become more relaxed. You no longer feel something unfair happened. You're no longer afraid of what's going to happen. Your body may have discomfort or pain, but *you* are comfortable. Body Comfortable means body relaxed. Work with it. Body relaxed is endless. Start wherever you can, but don't stop. Relax until body is relaxed, mind is relaxed, and emotions are relaxed. All relaxed means all present. That's Body Comfortable.

Start where you are, and move step by step. Every principle of Breema is endless, but also directional. That means there is always something you can do. If you forget the word "small," you'll never understand Breema. You can always take one small step. This understanding is sacred. We usually make a big aim for ourselves and never do it. But something small you may do. That gives you direction. Take one small step every day.

The nature of Existence is Awareness. Awareness manifests as Consciousness, energy, and matter. These four dimensions are the reality of your existence. If you look at yourself only as matter and energy, you become confused.

Everything that exists is made of these four dimensions. When you understand that, it becomes obvious that you don't need to do anything for the recipient. By you simply being present, the recipient benefits. When the sun is shining, you are welcome to stand in the sunlight or not. If you do, the sun doesn't think you owe it something. And if you don't, it doesn't get upset. If you think you are giving something, you may even get mad at someone for not receiving your "gift" and getting "healed." What kind of giving is that?

Breema helps you let go of those ideas. What remains is an atmosphere of acceptance, in which both you and the recipient are included. What makes you a good practitioner is body-mind connection and your receptivity to what is taking place in the moment. You no longer identify with Breema as "yours" when you understand that it's an expression of the unity of Existence, which is ever-present, every moment, everywhere. Of course, you can receive that emanation when you are receptive, but you don't claim it as your own. You yourself are a part of that undivided whole.

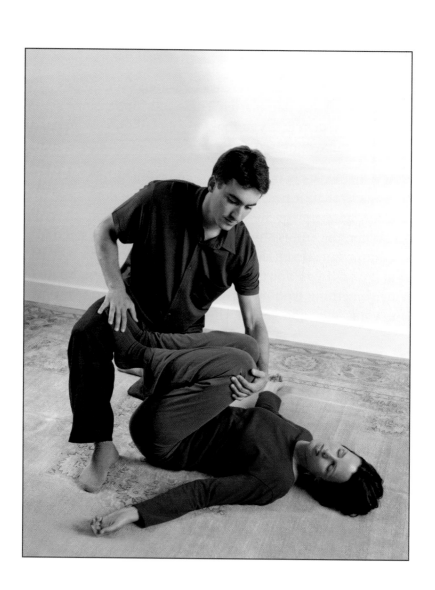

There is one Existence, one Consciousness, one life. Every time you practice Breema, you have an opportunity to come to yourself. If you're free from ideas, there is room for you to receive Conscious energy. When Conscious energy is there, there is connection.

When body, mind, and feelings are unified, you are present, and manifest what is needed. When you are in harmony with yourself, you are in harmony with your surroundings, and with all life. It's as simple as that.

In Breema, the direction is always from complication towards simplicity, from diversity towards unity. That's the direction for your entire life! There is one inclusive Existence, which even includes your thoughts and emotions. Everything belongs, but in its own dimension. You don't have to fight with your thoughts, you don't have to fight with your emotions. Let them be; let them come and go in their own dimension. *Your* dimension is the consciousness of *I exist*.

The Emphasis Is on Vitality

There's no diagnosis in Breema bodywork, because according to the philosophy of Breema, there is no such thing as disease. In the absence of vitality, we experience illness. So the emphasis is on vitality. In the same way, there is no darkness. In the absence of light, we experience darkness. Darkness has no substance of its own. But light has its own substance. Vitality has its own substance.

So in practicing Breema, you don't need to do anything for or to the recipient's body to make them healthy. In their actual existence, the recipient is healthy. They may not know it, but through the atmosphere of acceptance that's created, the recipient may receive a taste of their own essential vitality.

Because we think we are this body, our life is fear-based. We think that because of this body, we exist.

Breema supports us to come to the bigger picture. Through the taste of being present, we can see we are not this body.

This planet Earth is not separated from the rest of the universe. It is a school. When you come to the school of the Earth, you wear a uniform—this body. And when you are finished with this school, you leave your uniform behind. We identify with this uniform, and become frightened of everything, because anything could hurt this body. But nobody can hurt *you*.

When you see that you are not this body, you can enter a new dimension of consciousness in which you are free from identification with the body. You can see the body as a tool that you can use to fulfill your purpose.

All extra belongs to the past and future. No Extra means to become present. Whatever you don't need in this moment is extra. However much of that you can leave behind is in the right direction. That which you can do towards being present takes you where you need to go, provided you do it. The wisdom of your life is in doing the little things you can do.

When you *taste* your existence, you see you never before knew what you wanted in life. You wanted something, and later something else. But when you have a taste, you know you want that—to taste the reality of yourself. Because that gives you a moment of freedom from your conditioning.

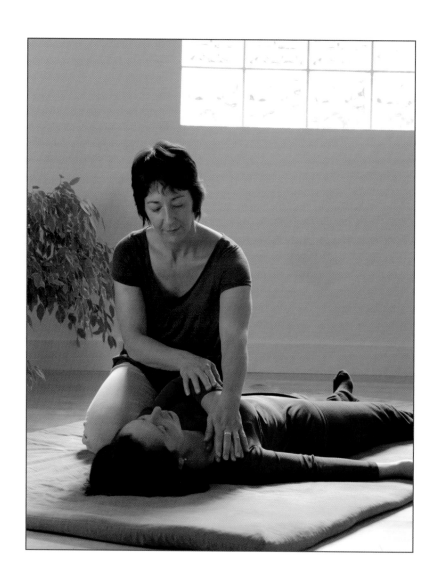

When you are practicing Breema, the more receptive you are, the more you become like an empty cup, ready to be filled up with Consciousness. You only need to let go of extra. The more you let go of self-image, the simpler you become. The direction is always from complication towards simplicity—from what you think you are to what you really are. That's why we say, "Breema is you yourself." You do Breema bodywork in order to move in that direction.

The bodywork sequences are just stations along the way, something to help you. Once you know them well, you don't need to focus on them. When you really know something, you don't have to hold it in your memory, because it becomes a part of you. Your own existence is also like that. When you really get a taste of it, and you come to that taste enough, you are not worried about who you are or what you are. You know you are part of one unified Existence. Your home is the entire cosmos, and you belong.

The creative energy of the universe is not in things. It's in the *relationship* between them. It's not in that which can be observed and identified. For example, in the principle of Firmness and Gentleness, firmness is not that creative energy. Neither is gentleness. But the relationship between them is in a higher dimension. That's the creative energy, and it includes both firmness and gentleness.

We practice Self-Breema to come to *taste*. When you have taste, stay with it and do your daily activities. Wash your face, brush your teeth, make a phone call—these become your Self-Breema.

If I'm identified with myself as something separate from the rest of Existence when I do Breema, what is it I'm doing? If I am separate, then I must be "somebody." Then I think "my" hand is doing Breema. If this hand is doing Breema, where is the rest of Existence? How could any separated phenomenon have reality?

Meaning Lives in the Present Moment

We do Breema to have tastes of being present. Then we need to find taste in our life. To the extent we are present, our life supports us instead of draining us. Meaningful life is very joyful. One of the reasons we always chase after all kinds of rewards is that we've lost the meaning. We can't find it in memory, in the past or future. Meaning lives in the present moment. And being in the moment doesn't take a philosophical quest. Just be yourself right now. The body breathes, and you know it. The body is manifesting. If you let go of your ideas of the future, and your stories about the past, you'll see that the body is manifesting in accord with certain principles—the Nine Principles of Harmony.

What you think you are causes you problems, no matter how you think of yourself. Because you are not your thoughts. Thought doesn't know you. Whenever you listen to your thoughts, they're giving you wrong advice, because they don't know you. In the absence of identification with thoughts and feelings, you get a glimpse of who you are. Thoughts can come and go. There's no problem there. But you don't have to believe them. In truth, you know yourself. You don't have to go ask your mind. You are that which *is*. It's that simple. There is one Existence. Existence is manifesting itself in the form of "you," and also as everything else that exists.

You are doing Breema. How much of you is participating? The more you do Breema with your whole body/whole mind, the more you let go of the imaginary concepts that limit you. When you have a moment of Full Participation, the entirety is doing Breema. Existence is manifesting itself.

The essential qualities we wish for are properties of *Being*. Being understands, Being loves, Being is compassionate, Being forgives. We hear or read about these qualities and we try to "do" them. But the "you" that tries to do them doesn't exist in the first place. We try to do things in our mind, as if the thought of them is sufficient. Thoughts are hollow. Substance has to flow through them from your Being. Being-participation gives substance to thoughts. The same for your feelings and your body. They are just vehicles through which your Being can express Conscious energy.

Should you try to do Breema with Conscious energy? No, because you can't. Do you need ideas? Do you need to do a "good job"? We don't really know what that means. So leave it alone. There's only one thing you can do. You can let go of extra. When you do Breema, let go of extra. That's all.

When you are present, your mind is where your body is. But if you look, you'll almost always find that your mind is everywhere but with the body.

When you are in the receptive state, your mind is with the activity of your body, and your feelings are supporting that connection. That way, you can experience your relationship to any of the Nine Principles while you're doing Breema. That's how you establish an actual relationship to your body.

If you just take the body to be what your eyes see, it's like looking at a cup without seeing that it's filled up with water. Through Breema, you experience the water in the cup by coming to the taste of *there is a body*.

Taste is available only in a moment of being present. When you have it, you see it is not dependent on the temporary condition of the body. Your perception of the body's condition is in thoughts, feelings, and sensations. But the body is matter, energy, Consciousness, and Awareness. It has an eternal dimension, not just the temporary characteristics we identify with. Taste connects you to that eternal dimension, and you have taste only when you are present.

Begin Where You Are

You are on this Earth to develop. To some degree, nature develops you, but you have to participate in your own completion.

If you look at your behavior, you can see that you are reacting to life, not living it. Being-participation is needed to really live life. The direction is to bring the mind to the body, and keep that connection until the feelings also come in.

Your body is manifesting. But that's not the body in your head. It's not the body you think you have. It's not even the body you see with your eyes. The body is a particle of the entirety. So, in truth, when body manifests, the entirety is supporting that manifestation. You can know that within yourself. In your understanding, you can connect everything that exists together in one whole unified Existence. And that's where you exist. As long as you take yourself to be separate, you don't really exist. Nothing exists as a separated something. If you look at your hand as just a hand, you don't see it's part of the totality of the body. Everything is one organic whole that belongs to a greater whole. When you do Breema, you need to have a taste of your own existence, which is in the Totality.

Breema always begins with connection. You bring your mind to the experience of the body. Then, throughout the session, you keep returning to the connection between body and mind.

It's simple, but you need to work with it until you taste it. That's when you know what body-mind connection means. The body and the mind we think we have don't really exist. We've been conditioned to think the body is an object that we can know by looking in a mirror. But the body isn't just an object—it has life. The mind isn't just a house of thoughts. When mind, body, and feelings are united in a common aim, they invite the Conscious energy we need in order to see.

What is it you see? You see how you are. You gain some self-knowledge. You have to constantly come back to yourself in order to eventually have Self-understanding.

We believe the universe is what our senses tell us, but our senses never perceive reality. Yet it is possible to understand, to relate to reality in understanding. The thing to do is to begin where you are. Body is manifesting. Bring the mind to be with the body. Then at some point, the feelings come in.

"I wish to be present." You wish that in order to be free from the past and future. Past and future are your interpretation of life, not life itself. If you look at your past, you find a lot of memories, haphazardly collected. None are exact. None are accurate. You don't live your life fully because you're always occupied with the past and future.

But there is a possibility—be present with the activity of the body, whatever you're doing, wherever you are. The reason you practice Breema bodywork is to have tastes of your own existence. When you know what taste is, you can take Breema to your daily life, so you can have the possibility to have taste when you walk, when you're on the phone, when you're sitting at the computer.

When you are fully participating, you receive life energy from your interactions. When you're not, you're just going through life mechanically. You have to be connected to the body—you have to be present in it. You have to be home. If you ask yourself "Where am I?" you'll see you're not home. But when mind, feelings, and body are together, you are at home.

*The taste of **there is a body***
is not a taste of something.
That taste itself is the body.
And it is our connection
to everything that exists.

When You Move Your Hand, the Entirety Is Moving

When you practice Breema, you may think your hand is moving, or maybe even that your body is moving. But there is *one* life, *one* energy, *one* Consciousness, *one* Awareness. When you move your hand, the entirety is moving.

What you observe with your senses are time-space events, and their measurement is by time and space. But taking that as the whole thing is like taking matter by itself to be reality. We forget about the intelligence of the architect that built this house, so we think the house is just wood, nails, mortar, and paint. We think we have this body because we ate food. We take the body to be separate from our consciousness, but it can't be separated.

You need to be available to yourself by being present—then Breema becomes Breema. When you touch the recipient, you are saying yes to the entirety.

The Nine Principles are present in every touch, every movement, provided you are present. You don't need to be anywhere else. The next second your mind may ask, "Did I pay my phone bill?" What's the problem with that? That's how the mind is. So it goes off to see if you've paid your bill. Do you need to go with it? Do you need to identify with the thoughts in your head? Aren't they just thoughts? There are thoughts, but you can still be present. Now, doing Breema becomes an expression of the present moment.

The highest gift you can offer to another person is to invite them to your innermost table. That's the table of being present. When you are present, you invite them to your table, as simple as that. Whether or not they come to the present is not your business. Your business is being present. That's all.

Look at a cherry tree filled up with cherries. Some are ripe, some are a day or two away, and some will ripen in a few weeks. Are you mad at the cherries that aren't ripe, or sad for them? The tree of life is just like that cherry tree. We are all in different stages. We all ripen in due time. You can't force someone to ripen. You allow them to be. Really, your business is with yourself.

You can taste any of the Nine Principles
in the taste of being present.
That's how you know them —
*with **Being**-knowledge.*

From Diversity Towards Unity

We are tense because we're not here, not in the body. We are not present. That's the root of tension.

Breema shows you how to become present. To be present, you have to not be in the past or future. There are two roads you can travel on. One is from complication towards simplicity. The other is from diversity towards unity.

To travel on these roads, Breema gives you the Nine Principles of Harmony to work with.

You're doing Breema. When your hand is on the recipient's shoulder, for example, that's the only thing you're doing. The next movement will take care of itself. But now is not next. This is Single Moment/Single Activity. It's connected to No Hurry/No Pause. When you experience being in the present moment, you don't feel pulled to indulge in the past or worry about the future.

The Entire Universe
Is Supporting This One Activity

If you understand the principle of Mutual Support, you can see that when you do Breema, the trillions of cells of your body are supporting. That's just to begin with. If you go a step deeper, you can see that the carpet, the walls, and the atmosphere are supporting.

If you let go of your crystallized thoughts and feelings, you will see that nothing can manifest unless the Totality is manifesting. So everything in the entire universe is supporting this one activity.

Can you experience this? You can. Let go of the concepts of "me" and "mine" and the entire cosmos becomes your home. You become all that exists, and at the same time, part of all that exists. This is the only real meaning of the word "exists." You can't separate something from the whole and say it exists. Then it only has imaginary existence, because separation takes place in an imaginary world. In the world of reality, there is only unity.

So don't take this principle lightly. At the same time, be light when you are working with it. Mutual Support is a natural phenomenon. Your only obstacles are what's been put in your mind. But there is no obstacle separating you from Existence, because Existence has already accepted you as you are.

When you are present, there is perfect mutual support—you are both active and receptive at the same time. Mutual Support allows you to support yourself, moment after moment.

Body-mind connection is not just a phrase. It's not something you can just think of and have. It's a particular taste.

When you practice Breema, there can be no expectation, no thought of healing or balancing the recipient. You practice for one purpose only— to bring your mind to the activity of your body. As you continue, you become more balanced, because the relationship between mind, feelings, and body becomes more balanced.

The mind is outwardly oriented. It relates to everything through interpretation of what the sense organs receive. As soon as you look at something, your mind starts to make commentary.

When you come to a balanced state, the mind can receive from your consciousness. Then you have a grain of Conscious energy. Consciousness has light, and with that light, it penetrates and sees through, so you can see where you are.

If, for example, you see that you're imbalanced, it means there is some degree of balance too, otherwise you couldn't see that. By accepting what you see, your energy can support balance.

You are not harmed by what you see of yourself with acceptance. *Seeing* means coming out of the periphery of the mind, which is filled up with concepts mechanically acquired from mass consciousness. These concepts make you perceive life in a fragmented way. But in seeing, you are no longer limited by preconceptions and unverified thoughts. You see with the light provided by your consciousness, and because your wish is to see things as they are in reality, you are nurtured by the fact that you see.

When you fully accept something, you don't have to react to it anymore.

How do you know that what you're doing is Breema? When the mind is connected to the body, you're doing Breema. This is not your usual mind. The mind that's interested in being with the body creates friendship with the body. That friendship invites your feelings. When body, mind, and feelings are together, there is a sense of presence.

Breema is not about what you do, nor even about how you are. It's about the fact that you *are*.

You Have the Possibility to Know Yourself

Practicing Breema helps you to see you need to be present. The recipient is supporting you by giving you an opportunity to practice.

The aim of Breema runs through every aspect of the bodywork. Always keep the aim paramount. Everything you do in Breema is for the purpose of Self-understanding.

The more you connect to this aim, the more free you become. You know what you need to do. When you move away from it, you become confused. You always know what you're supposed to do when you're on the right track. And the only possibility of knowing is in Self-understanding.

If you try to help the recipient, you can never be sure you are helping. You can never know the recipient, what's going to happen to them, or what experiences they need to go through in life. But you have the possibility to know yourself. You can help yourself by becoming present. And helping yourself is the best way to help the recipient. Breema is rooted in the interrelatedness and interconnectedness of everything that exists.

You don't need to look at people the way they may look at themselves. Don't think of them the way they think of themselves. No matter how they present themselves physically, mentally, or emotionally, something real is also there. Practicing Breema, you relate to that which is real by becoming present.

When we bring body, mind, and feelings together, we discover that we are not our body, mind, or feelings. We are that which is conscious of them.

As you continue to work with the aim of being present, you eventually see that it's no longer this hand doing Breema, nor just that shoulder receiving what your hand is doing. Everything is in unity. At some point, the word "me" disappears. You see there is not some "you" that exists. There is only one whole Existence manifesting itself. There is nobody there to take credit, and nobody there to take blame. If blame goes, judgment goes with it. If credit goes, possessiveness goes with it. Then we simply *are*, manifested aspects of one whole unified Existence. We are part of Existence. We're no longer "homeless." The entire cosmos is our home.

Breema is about self-transformation. The self-transformation that takes place in a timeless moment in which you let go of mechanical consciousness and taste body-mind connection, or taste *I exist,* is true alchemy.

Breema is meant to be practiced in full simplicity. There is no separation. You are in unity with the recipient and with Existence. The body is Existence manifesting itself. It is the Timeless appearing in time, and it never loses its Timeless nature. You don't have to do something to make it so—it is already so. Your doing is only to help you to let go of your identification, so you can come to the dimension in which you see things as they really are.

Your Thoughts
Are Just Thoughts

Things come as they come, and go as they go. It's like sitting in a movie theater. Images appear on the screen. All of a sudden, you see a ferocious fire start, and it burns everything. Later on, you see a flood that washes everything away. When the movie ends, the screen is still there, and it's still white. It didn't get burned. It didn't get wet. That's how the events of life are. They come and go.

If you look, you'll see that usually you're having an argument with someone, criticizing something, or commenting about something. And you don't know that all of it is taking place in your thoughts.

If you bring body and mind together and come to the active state, you have a chance to see that your thoughts are just thoughts, just images that come and go. Your feelings are just images. What do they have to do with you? The events of life come and go, but you are not obligated to go with them. Let them come, let them go, while you remain present with your body. When body, mind, and feelings are together, you are unified within yourself. In that unity, you become unified with all that exists. There is one whole unified Existence. Nothing exists as a separate thing. Everything is interconnected, interrelated.

Full Participation means body, mind, and feelings together are participating. When you are fully participating, there is no extra.

In fact, when you apply any of the Nine Principles, there is No Extra, No Force, No Judgment, No Hurry/No Pause. These four are always included in any of the Nine Principles you work with. You have an image of yourself. To begin to see through your self-image, you have to put these four "no" principles into practice. If you practice them enough, you become convinced that you really are judgmental, that you always have extra, that you're always hurrying and hesitating, and that you always use force. As that becomes clear to you, you can benefit more from the other five principles. Then when you say Body Comfortable, you're not referring to the body that's part of your self-image, because the four "no" principles have helped you lessen your identification with self-image. Then your body is comfortable, and you know what body means, because you have a *taste*. Whenever you let go of your self-image, you really can fully participate, you really can have Single Moment/Single Activity. When you place your hand on the recipient's instep, you're not putting your hand there in order to then move it somewhere else. *This is it.* When you do move your hand to the ankle, then again, this is it. That's how you can understand Single Moment/Single Activity—by taste.

If there is no self-image, there is no separation, and everything you do is Mutual Support. Life is giving to life. Existence is manifesting itself. You become more free from "me" and "mine."

You can only know the Nine Principles by taste, not by anything else. And to taste them, you have to put them into practice in your daily life. Then you will see for yourself what a gift the Nine Principles are to your life.

Moment after moment,
the emanation of the Absolute
passes through everything that exists.
When we receive it, we are present.

From Complication Towards Simplicity

Everything has a relationship to the Absolute and manifests based on that relationship. The diversity of relative existence means that there are many dimensions of consciousness, each with a different ability to see beyond the appearance of phenomena and recognize their actual meaning. The finer or "higher" the level of consciousness, the greater the ability to see things as they actually are—in unity—interrelated, interconnected, all arising from the same source.

Once this really makes sense to you, you begin to wish to raise your level of consciousness. If this becomes your aim, it gives purpose and meaning to your life.

You have a direction. You begin to appreciate people who have the same aim as you—to lessen identification with the acquired aspect. As meaning and purpose grow in your life, identification lessens.

Working with the Nine Principles helps you move from diversity towards unity, from complication towards simplicity. Each principle is an expression of your True nature.

As you practice the principles, they become practical knowledge for practical application in your everyday life. They help you live your life more meaningfully.

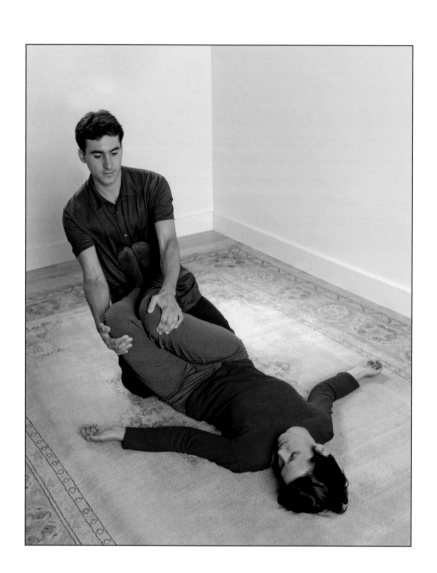

To do Breema, you don't need to be knowledgeable. You don't need to be dexterous. You don't need to help the recipient, or balance them or heal them. When you try to do that, you are in the dark, in confusion, because you don't know what helping the recipient means. What kind of help do you want to give? Some idea you read about? Some idea that came from a previous experience?

What if your aim becomes to let go of that for a few minutes? Then you see you don't know how to let go. Seeing that is valuable. You can't tell your mind to not think, or your feelings to be present or balanced.

So what to do? Come to this earth—this body. You have a body. Experience it, know it, be with it. Know it in such a way your mind remains with it.

The practice of Breema is based on bringing body and mind together. You can practice that in everything. When you walk, when you eat, when you're on the phone, you could bring body and mind together.

If you practice that enough, you will find some balance in your life. Your mind doesn't automatically run all over the place, because you have body-mind connection.

You Are Not What
You Think You Are

By practicing Self-Breema you may see that every movement of your body could be Self-Breema. Self-Breema is any movement of the body that connects you to yourself. And when you get connected, you see that you are you and *not* you at the same time. Your identification with your personal name and your personal life and your personal opinions slowly lessens as you see that only the Totality exists.

Every cell in your body indicates one thing—that your body exists. In the same way, everything that exists announces the existence of an intelligence that is the source of all life. Everything comes from the Absolute. Everything is light. Everything comes from light and returns to light. Not the reflected light we see with our eyes. It's the light of Awareness, the light of Being-existence, the intelligence of the universe.

Bringing body and mind together is a good starting point. The mind should be where the body is. You tame your mind by creating a relationship between it and the body. Eventually, that body-mind connection becomes one particle of Consciousness. That's the direction, the way to begin fulfilling your potential to live your life consciously.

Self-Breema starts with the Self-Breema exercises you learn. Those are to help you get a taste of what Body Comfortable means. Then you can take the principles into your daily life and begin working with them. You could walk with Body Comfortable. You could pick up a telephone with No Extra. Slowly, your whole life could become a field in which you practice Self-Breema. Washing your hands is an opportunity to become present. You could shake hands with someone, without trying to make a statement. Knowing what your body is doing without describing or evaluating it supports you to become present.

You can have only one teacher in your life, not two. And that is you, yourself. You can learn only from yourself. Of course, we always need the support of those who have greater Self-understanding. But the bottom line is, each of us has to wake up within our self.

When you do Breema, you are not led by associative thoughts and ideas. With the wisdom that becomes available through body-mind connection, you simply respond instead of reacting.

You place your hand on the recipient's body. That hand is not a separate phenomenon. It's an aspect of your body. Your body isn't a separate phenomenon either. It's an aspect of your consciousness. Nor is your consciousness a separate phenomenon. It's the emanation of Awareness, of the Totality of everything that exists. Because of this, the body is also in unity with all that exists—it's also the emanation of Awareness.

Don't get stuck in your crystallized concepts about the body. The body is not what you think it is. Neither are you! You are not what you think you are. Nothing is what you think it is. As soon as you identify with the thought of something, you become blind to that actual phenomenon. You can't see it. It's fine to have thoughts, but you have to see that they are just thoughts, not reality.

If you practice Breema and the Nine Principles enough, the inner aspect of you receives it, and it becomes your inner atmosphere. Then as soon as you begin to do Breema or Self-Breema, that atmosphere can become available to you. Then, instead of manifesting from your mechanical consciousness, you can manifest with the energy that's connected to a higher dimension within yourself. When you're connected to that, you grow. Your consciousness becomes finer.

When you practice Breema, drop your desire to help. Don't look at the recipient as someone who has something wrong with them and needs your help. You and the recipient are simply receivers of one universal energy that supports you both. That's why you don't need to judge them. You don't need to fix them.

If you try to help the recipient, you are moving in the wrong direction, because you can never know just what they need. But you do know what you need. You need to become present and remain present. That's the only way you can really help the recipient—by helping yourself. They are welcome to benefit as much as you. Breema offers both of you an opportunity to let go of some of your identification. The less identification, the more it's possible to accept things as they are. In acceptance, body, mind, and feelings are supported to come to balance and harmony.

To Be Receptive,
Your Being Has to Participate

To be connected to the recipient, you first have to be connected to yourself. So your aim should be to bring body and mind together, and stay with that until your feelings join in. Then body, mind, and feelings are participating together in harmony. When you are connected to yourself, you become connected to all that is.

Our relationships deteriorate and become problematic because that connection isn't there. When you are not connected to yourself, you don't know how to connect to someone else. Instead of connecting, you react. Reaction causes another reaction, and no one understands anyone else. Body-mind connection takes you out of reactive life and brings you to active life. You have to become active in order to enter receptive life. When body, mind, and feelings are united, functioning as one, you are receptive.

You begin to experience the value of practicing Breema when you're in the active state. If you do it in the passive state, it doesn't mean much. It may relax you or the recipient a bit, but nothing has real value unless it touches your Being. Breema has one purpose—to touch your Being.

Breema is to connect you to the meaning and purpose of your life. It does that by helping you bring mind, feelings, and body together. You work with Breema to move from the passive state to the active state, and from the active state to the receptive state. To be receptive, your

Being has to participate. And we don't know what Being is. It can't be conceptualized. You can't understand it mentally. You have to be it.

When you come to the active state, Breema starts to become Breema. Body and mind work together. In each moment, the Nine Principles are manifesting. Your body is comfortable. How do you know? Because you have body-mind connection. Body-mind connection is Body Comfortable, No Extra, Full Participation, Mutual Support, and all of the other principles. One of the principles may be more apparent to you, but they are all there.

You may have a taste of being present. That taste can become something you trust, something you know you wish.

Your hand cannot be separate from your consciousness. In the receptive state, you can receive Conscious energy. But receptivity can't be forced. It's given when you have a correct relationship to yourself.

BREEMA

Being

Right now

Everywhere

Every moment

Myself

Actually

The Breema Center

Since 1980, the Breema Center has been presenting Breema's practical approach to harmony and Self-understanding. The world headquarters for practitioner and instructor certification and continuing education, the Center also gives classes, workshops, and intensives for beginning, intermediate, and advanced students. People come from all over the world, attracted by Breema's philosophy, principles, bodywork, and exercises. Studying at the Center, they find essential support in creating a new, unified relationship between the body, mind, and feelings, and in bringing greater harmony and presence to their lives.

The Breema Center maintains an active relationship with certified practitioners and instructors, and an up-to-date international directory of instructors and practitioners, plus listings of Breema classes and presentations worldwide. Information is available on our website, by phone, or mail.

THE BREEMA CENTER
Jon Schreiber, D.C., Director
6076 Claremont Avenue
Oakland, CA 94618

510-428-0937
800-452-1008
fax: 510-428-9235
e-mail: center@breema.com
website: www.breema.com

The Breema Clinic

We have been using Breema bodywork, Self-Breema exercises, and working with the principles of Breema since 1981 to support people to experience greater well-being, harmony, and essential interest in life. Receiving Breema and practicing Self-Breema support the unification of body, mind, and feelings. As these three come together, they begin to function naturally, and we become receptive to finer consciousness. This becomes our entry to *real* health, which means harmony with Existence.

THE BREEMA CLINIC
Jon Schreiber, D.C., Director
6201 Florio Street
Oakland, CA 94618

phone: 510-428-1234
fax: 510-428-2705

email: clinic@breema.com
website: www.breemahealth.com

Jon Schreiber

Jon Schreiber is the director of the Breema Center, the world headquarters for teaching Breema and certifying Breema practitioners and instructors. He is also the founder and director of the Breema Clinic in Oakland, California, which focuses on the transformational tools of Breema, Self-Breema, and the Nine Principles of Harmony in supporting people to move in the direction of real health and a more purposeful and meaningful life. Since 1980 he has been teaching at the Breema Center, as well as nationally and internationally, and is the author of many books on the philosophy, principles, and practice of Breema.

Books & CDs from Breema Center Publishing

For reading...

BREEMA *and the Nine Principles of Harmony*

BY JON SCHREIBER • $25.00 hardcover, 168 pages, 7" x 9", 81 photos

Breema is universal and has great potential value to anyone with a sincere interest in Truth, because it's a practical road to Self-understanding. Breema's timeless principles are applicable to every situation in life, and they open us to the possibility of awakening to the essential unity of Existence in this very moment.

SELF-BREEMA: *Exercises for Harmonious Life, Second Edition*

BY JON SCHREIBER & DENISE BEREZONSKY • $29.95 hardcover, 246 pages, 8½" x 11", 39 photos, 400+ illustrations

41 fully illustrated Self-Breema exercises and an introduction to Breema's Nine Principles of Harmony. Practicing Self-Breema helps us move in unity with the natural laws that govern life and health, and live in balance with ourselves, others, and all life.

Freedom Comes from Understanding: *Insights for Meaningful Life*

BY JON SCHREIBER • $18.00 hardcover, 200 pages, 4½" x 6"

How does Existence support you? By letting you know you belong. When you become conscious of your own existence, that Consciousness is the beginning of connection to your Timeless nature.

Every Moment Is Eternal: *The Timeless Wisdom of Breema*

BY JON SCHREIBER • $15.00 hardcover, 200 pages, 4½" x 6"

This book talks to our essential nature, because Truth already exists there. The more our essence is nurtured, the greater the chance that cracks may appear in our conditioned attitude towards life. Through these cracks, we may see things we haven't seen before, and nourish our essential desire for Self-understanding.

Freedom Is in *This* Moment: *365 Insights for Daily Life*

BY JON SCHREIBER • $18.95 hardcover, 448 pages, 4½" x 6"

When you read these writings, you are filled up with an inner resonance, because their reality and meaning are in you as well as all around you. When you hear the Truth, you also hear it inside of yourself, in your very essence. The Truth is not something foreign. It's already part of you just because you exist!

For listening...

With our audio books on disc, you can be nurtured by the atmosphere of Breema wherever you have a CD player. Choose an excerpt, or listen from beginning to end.

Waking Up to This Moment:
The Essential Meaning of Breema
READ BY JON SCHREIBER
$20 for the 2-CD set

BREEMA *and the*
Nine Principles of Harmony
READ BY JON SCHREIBER
$20 for the 2-CD set

Freedom Comes from Understanding:
Insights for Meaningful Life
READ BY JON SCHREIBER
$20 for the 2-CD set

Order Breema books and audio CDs from our website!

10% off the cover price
free domestic shipping
www.breema.com
(click on **BOOKSTORE**)

The Breema Center • 6076 Claremont Ave • Oakland, CA 94618
800.452.1008 • 510.428.0937 • center@breema.com